THE EIGHT
BEATITUDES

By
REV. LAWRENCE G. LOVASIK, S.V.D.
Divine Word Missionary

NIHIL OBSTAT; Daniel V. Flynn, J.C.D., *Censor Librorum*
IMPRIMATUR: ✝ Joseph T. O'Keefe, D.D., *Vicar General, Archdiocese of New York*

Catholic Book Publishing Corp., NJ   ISBN 978-0-89942-384-5

THE EIGHT BEATITUDES

THE BEATITUDES announce happiness for those who want to serve God. They are the ways by which we can live a good Christian life and avoid the false teaching of the world. We can be holy and pleasing to God if we live according to the Beatitudes which Jesus spoke about in His Sermon on the Mount.

After Jesus had chosen His twelve Apostles, He wanted to teach them how to do His work of bringing people to God. Up the mountainside they climbed. Then Jesus sat down, and they gathered near to hear Him. Many others were listening to the words which Jesus spoke.

In this wonderful Sermon Jesus taught how Christians should live, how they should pray, how they should treat their enemies and their friends, how God loves and cares for them.

Jesus began to teach the crowds:

"HOW blest are the poor in spirit:
the reign of God is theirs.
Blest are the sorrowing; they shall be consoled.
Blest are the lowly; they shall inherit the land.
Blest are they who hunger and thirst for holiness;
they shall have their fill.
Blest are they who show mercy;
mercy shall be theirs.
Blest are the single-hearted
for they shall see God.
Blest are the peacemakers; they shall be called sons
of God.
Blest are those persecuted for holiness' sake;
the reign of God is theirs."

Jesus Teaches Us
How to Come to Heaven

WHEN Jesus finished His Sermon, He
said:

"So then, everyone who hears these words
of mine and obeys them will be like a wise
man who built his house on the rock. The rain
poured down, the rivers flooded over and the
winds blew hard against that house. But it did
not fall, because it had been built on the rock.

"But everyone who hears these words of Mine, and does not obey them will be like a foolish man who built his house on the sand. The rain poured down, the rivers flooded over, the winds blew hard against that house, and it fell. What a terrible fall that was!"

The people looked at each other in surprise. Surely Jesus was the greatest teacher of all. His words were the words of God.

Those who loved God wanted to live by these words. Jesus told them that God would help them.

The Beatitudes point out the way to heaven. If we live according to them we shall be happy in this world and also in heaven.

We should pray to Jesus that He might help us to understand His teaching and to practice it in our daily lives.

Jesus Wants Me to Trust in God

IN the Eight Beatitudes Jesus teaches us to put our trust in God, our heavenly Father, like a child trusts its father on earth. He said: "Unless you become as little children, you cannot enter the kingdom of heaven."

Jesus promised in the Beatitudes that our heavenly Father would reward us in heaven if we live according to His teaching in the Gospel. He said: "Be glad and rejoice, for your reward is great in heaven."

When we trust in God we can live as peacefully as a child asleep in bed who trusts in the love of its parents.

THE FIRST BEATITUDE

"How blest are the poor in spirit: the reign of God is theirs." — *Mt 5:3*

JESUS, You teach me
that I shall reach the Kingdom of Heaven
if I am poor in spirit.
Like You I must look
for the riches of heaven
and not for those that pass away.

Jesus, You taught us
that we will be truly rich
if we have God's grace in our soul.
Grace makes my soul holy
and pleasing to God.

You said: "What profit does a man show
who gains the whole world
and destroys himself in the process?

What can a man offer in exchange for his
life?"

Paul knows that to be poor in spirit he must do God's will rather than his own. He keeps the Fourth Commandment of God by obeying his mother who told him to clean up the yard and cut the grass.

Jesus Gives Me Grace

JESUS, I receive Your grace
    when I go to confession
and ask pardon for my sins
in the Sacrament of Penance.

I receive grace when I receive You
in the Sacrament of the Holy Eucharist.
Holy Communion is my greatest Treasure
because I receive You into my heart.

I receive Your grace when I pray
because I am united with You by love.
Teach me to pray often during the day
so that I may ever be close to You.

Jesus, make me poor in spirit
by putting my trust in You.
I can do nothing good by myself;
I need Your help to be good.

I ask for Your grace
that I may live as a child of God,
and the Kingdom of heaven will be mine.

THE SECOND BEATITUDE

"Blest too are the sorrowing; they shall be consoled."

JESUS, Your Beatitude teaches me
to be truly sorry for my sins
because they have offended You,
who are the highest Good.

When I see You hanging on the Cross,
let me remember that my sins
have caused You much pain.
I am sorry for having hurt You so much.

Help me to show that I am truly sorry
by keeping away from sin
and by receiving the Sacrament of Penance
as often as I can.

Richard and his sister Kathy go to confession at least each month. They tell God that they are sorry for their sins. God forgives them and He will bless them for having sorrow for their sins. He gives them His peace and joy.

Jesus Wants Me to Be Sorry

IF I have this kind of sorrow,
I can be sure that You will console me
and give me strength to avoid all sin.

Jesus, be with me when I am in pain
and when I am sick or sad about something.
I want to take my troubles to You
because I know that You will help me.
You are my dearest Friend.
and You will console me.

You once said;
"Come to Me, all you who are weary
and find life burdensome,
and I will refresh you."

When I find things hard to bear,
let me always say:
"All for You, O Sacred Heart of Jesus.
I trust in You."

THE THIRD BEATITUDE

"Blest are the lowly; they shall inherit the land."

— Mt 5:5

JESUS, You once said:
"Learn of Me, because I am gentle
and humble of heart,
and your souls will find rest."

I ask You to teach me
how to be humble like You
because only then can I reach heaven.

Help me to keep Your commandments
and follow Your way of life,
for You said that only then would I love You.

Jesus said that He came to serve and not to be served. Michael wants to be like Jesus helping his mother. He goes to the store for her and helps her around the house. He is happy because he can serve by being kind.

Jesus Wants Me to Obey

JESUS, You teach me in this Beatitude
that I am humble when I am obedient
to my parents and teachers
and listen to what they tell me to do
because they love me very much
and want what is best for me.

When I obey I shall be happy,
because I shall be like You.
You were always obedient to Your Father
and ever did His will.

Jesus, help me to be truly humble
by accepting all that happens to me
as coming from the hand of my heavenly
   Father,
who loves me more than anyone can.

Teach me to be patient and kind,
like a humble child of God,
for then I can be sure of having heaven
as my eternal reward.

THE FOURTH BEATITUDE

"Blest are they who hunger and thirst for holiness; they shall have their fill."

— Mt 5:6

JESUS, You once said:
  "I am the Way, the Truth, and the Life."
If I want to be holy,
I must follow Your example of goodness,
because You are the only true Way to God.

I must believe in Your word,
because You are the eternal Truth.
I must come to You for grace,
because all grace and holiness comes from
  You.

I really want to be holy.
I trust that You will give me the grace I need.

Bobby and his sister, Karen, receive Jesus in Holy Communion every Sunday, and sometimes during the week. Jesus feeds their soul with His Body and Blood. They have a great desire to be with Jesus.

Jesus Wants Me to Be Holy

JESUS, You teach me that I shall be holy
if I do the Will of God,
as You told us to pray:
"Thy will be done on earth
as it is in heaven."

You have always done Your Father's will.
Help me to do the same.

Jesus, Your Beatitude teaches me
to really want to be holy
and to strive to be good with all my strength.
You promised to give me the grace I need
through Your Sacraments and prayer.

I want to receive You in Holy Communion
often
to receive the grace to be kind
and pure and obedient and humble.

I want to pray often during the day
to get the help I need from You
to be more like You
and to be pleasing to my Heavenly Father.

THE FIFTH BEATITUDE

"Blest are they who show mercy; mercy shall be theirs."

JESUS, You came to this earth
to show us God's mercy
by giving Your life on the Cross
to take away our sins
and bring us to eternal life.

You said:
"God so loved the world
that He gave His only Son
that all who believe in Him
may have eternal life."

In this Beatitude You teach me
to be kind and merciful to others.
You said: "As often as you did it
for one of my least brothers,
you did it for Me."

Janet always forgives her playmates when they do something that she does not like. She never tries to get even when they hurt her. She knows that Jesus taught us to forgive others if we want God to forgive our sins.

Jesus Wants Me to Show Mercy

JESUS, I am a sinner
because I have often offended You.
You have shown Your mercy to me
by forgiving my sins
especially in the Sacrament of Penance.

Help me to be merciful to others
and forgive them when they hurt me,
that I may be forgiven by God,
for You taught us to pray:
"Forgive us our trespasses
as we forgive those
who trespass against us."

Give me the grace to show mercy,
that I may receive mercy from You.
I forgive all who have hurt me.
I beg You to forgive me.

THE SIXTH BEATITUDE

"Blest are the single-hearted for they shall see God."
— Mt 5:8

JESUS, in this Beatitude You teach us
that only those who are pure of heart
will see God in heaven.
It is only by Your grace
that I can keep my heart clean from sin.

Give me the help I need
to keep away from all that is evil
so that my soul may be pleasing to You
and that I may be Your Friend.

I want to receive Holy Communion often
and to pray often during each day
that I may be pure of heart
and be worthy to see God in heaven.

Billy has a classmate who sometimes uses bad language and looks at bad pictures. Billy will not look at a comic book which his classmate wants him to read because he knows it has bad pictures and words in it. He wants to be pure of heart that he might be a friend of Jesus.

Jesus Wants Me to Be Good

JESUS, You teach me to be single-hearted
by seeking God in everything I do,
by doing all for the love of Him.

I ask You for the grace
to love God with all my heart and soul
and to love people for His sake.

Jesus, You said of Your disciples:
"As the Father has loved Me,
so I have loved you.
Live on in My love.
You will live in My love
if you keep My commandments,
even as I have kept My Father's commandments,
and live in His love."

Jesus, help me to live in Your love,
by doing Your holy Will.

THE SEVENTH BEATITUDE

"Blest too the peacemakers; they shall be called sons of God." — *Mt 5:9*

JESUS, when You were born,
  angels sang in the sky:
"Glory to God in the high heavens,
peace on earth to those
on whom His favor rests."

By Your Death on the Cross
You made up for our sins
and brought us the peace of God's children.
You made peace between God and us.

You are the Savior of the world
and the Prince of Peace.
You are truly a peacemaker.

A peacemaker is one who tries to keep peace at home or after school. Marie wants to be a good child of God by helping her playmates and her brothers and sisters to love one another.

Jesus Wants Me to Seek Peace

JESUS, make me a peacemaker
and guide my actions in the way of peace.
Jesus, at the Last Supper You said:
"Peace is My farewell to you,
My peace is My gift to you.
I do not give it to you
as the world gives peace."

Give me the peace the world cannot give.
Help me to be at peace with God,
at peace with myself,
and at peace with all people around me.

I pray for peace in the world.
May people everywhere
live according to Your holy laws
that they may love each other in peace.

Jesus, keep me close to You,
and live in Your peace as a child of God.

THE EIGHTH BEATITUDE

"Blessed are those persecuted for holiness' sake; the reign of God is theirs."

—*Mt 5:10*

JESUS, You told Your Apostles
  that they would have to suffer for Your
sake.
You said: "You will suffer in the world.
But take courage! I have overcome the world."

Give me the grace to make sacrifices for my
  Faith,
and to prove my love for You
by being willing to suffer to save my soul.

You promised to help me to be brave
and patient in carrying my daily cross
because You have overcome the world.

Jimmy's schoolmates make fun of him because they see him blessing himself and saying a little prayer before eating his lunch in the school cafeteria. But Jimmy is brave. He shows his love for God by saying a meal prayer even when he is persecuted by his schoolmates.

Jesus Asks Me to Live for Him

JESUS, You gave Your life for me,
  so much did You love me.
I want to live my life for You
as a child of God and a true Christian.

Jesus, I pray for the many Christians
who are suffering for their Faith
in many parts of the world.
Give them Your courage and strength
that they may not be afraid
because You are always with them
to help them prove their love for You.

Jesus, may I and those I love
deserve the great reward You promised
to those who suffer for Your honor,
because You said: "Be glad and rejoice,
for your reward is great in heaven."

To see You forever in heaven
is our greatest reward.

When we pray, the Holy Spirit answers our prayer by giving us his grace.

HOLY Spirit, dearest Friend of my soul,
give me Your grace.
Help me to walk in faith
and grow in the strength of Your love
till I become more like Jesus.
May I live in holiness
according to the teaching of Jesus.

Peace

Prayer for Help
to Live According to the Beatitudes

JESUS, help me to be poor in spirit,
that I may seek heavenly riches
and not those that pass away with time.

Help me to be truly sorry for my sins,
that I may be forgiven by God.

Help me to want to be holy
by being united with You
through love in Holy Communion and prayer.